His Delight

31 Days of Praise & Worship

ADESHOLA EZEOKOLI

ISBN: 0-9831-2709-3
ISBN-13: 9780983127093

DEDICATION

*Dedicated
to
my lovely daughters,
Adora
and
Chimamanda*

ACKNOWLEDGEMENTS

I would like to acknowledge the men of God who have spoken into my life and given me an avenue to express the gifts of God in my life: Pastor Kayode Ijisesan, Pastor Gbade Ogunlana, Pastor Gary Clarke and Pastor Segun Oludipe.

I would like to acknowledge the Pastors and members of KingsWord International Church Chicago. You are a true spiritual family in every sense of the word. I would also like to acknowledge my immediate and extended family for all your love and support.

Last but not least, I would like to thank my husband, Dozie Ezeokoli, a true spiritual head who taught me so many things I know and who continually "pushes" me and guides me towards fulfilling my destiny in Christ.

TABLE OF CONTENTS

FOREWORD

Thou art worthy, O Lord, to receive glory and honour and power: for thou hast created all things, and for thy pleasure they are and were created.

(Revelation 4:11, KJV)

God created all things for His pleasure according to the above scripture. In other words, we exist to give pleasure to God. It has always been the will of God that man will forever be connected to Him. He created man in His image and according to His likeness so that we can extend His nature to our environment.

John 4:24 shows clearly that God is a spirit and that He can only be worshipped effectively in spirit and in truth. Every child of God has been recreated in His spirit so that the capacity to worship Him in spirit and in truth can be restored back to man. Man before the fall in the Garden of Eden had unrestricted fellowship with God. He connected to God without any hindrance or barrier.

However, the sin nature that dominated man since his fall from glory incapacitated his spirit and left him in a disconnected state.

1

The damage that sin brought to man was fixed through the death and resurrection of Jesus Christ of Nazareth. New Creation men and women have now been restored back into fellowship and true worship. We have now been adopted back into the family of God and are now in a position to cry 'Abba Father.' You don't have to stay in the outer court any longer.

By the blood of the lamb, you are now empowered to come boldly before God to receive grace and mercy at all times. You no longer need a high priest with human limitations to continually offer sacrifices on your behalf. Jesus, once and for all made an eternal sacrifice to bring us back home. We are indeed free to worship God in spirit and in truth. The intent of this book is to help you cultivate the habit of true worship. God is committed to the restoration of true worship in this generation.

I believe the singular purpose why God inspired the author to write this great piece is because he wants you to become addicted to His worship. The book has been designed in such a way that you can easily form a healthy habit of worship by dedicating a whole month to the study of God's Word on the subject. In as much as the fruit of our lips is a major part of worship, we must realize that worship is different from singing.

In fact, worship is more of a lifestyle than any other thing. God wants your whole life: spirit, soul and body to be consecrated to Him in worship.

He wants you to adore and revere Him with all He has given to you beyond just using the vehicle of music.

I beseech you therefore, brethren, by the mercies of God, that ye present your bodies a living sacrifice, holy, acceptable unto God, which is your reasonable service. And be not conformed to this world: but be ye transformed by the renewing of your mind, that ye may prove what is that good, and acceptable, and perfect, will of God.

(Romans 12:1-2, KJV)

Now is the time for unrestrained and undiluted worship. After all, everything we are and have originally belongs to God. I trust God that your revelation on worship will be upgraded as you diligently digest the content of this great piece. Remember, you are a part of 'the true worshipper' generation.

Kayode Ijisesan
Lead Pastor, KingsWord Everywhere

INTRODUCTION

❧

Praise means "to proclaim the glory of". Worship means "to offer honor or respect to someone as a divine power". Sometimes these words are used interchangeably. Praise and worship is not just about singing or dancing (although these are important).

It is also about a lifestyle that puts God above everything else in life and doing those things that truly bring glory to His name. Praise is about expressing joy over what God has done for you and worship is about acknowledging who God is: A Savior, a Father, a Friend, a Comforter, a Provider, a truly awesome and majestic One who is worthy of praise.

Praise brings God on the scene in your life and drives away the forces of darkness. Corporate praise, that is, a form of praise offered during worship services, if done right, creates an atmosphere for miracles, blessings, various anointings and direction from God.

(Isaiah 12:5-6) *Sing to the Lord, for he has done glorious things; let this be known to the world. Shout aloud and sing for joy, people of Zion for great is the Holy One of Israel among you.*

5

Besides singing songs of praise, there are certain other things that we do that bring glory and praise to the name of God. Some of them include sharing our faith with others, studying God's Word and developing a close relationship with Him; giving to God's work, and speaking words of faith.

This devotional will focus on specific acts of praise and worship. Some chapters will focus on the attitude we should have as people who would live a life of praise; whereas other chapters will focus on some down to earth, practical tips on how to live a better life of worship.

A few chapters will also focus on worshipping God in a congregational setting, as well as tips for leading worship. May the Lord of Heaven and earth bless you abundantly as He takes your worship and praise of Him to another level in Jesus' name, Amen!

⌒⌒ Day 1 ⌒⌒

THE HEART'S ATTITUDE

(Matthew 22:37) *Jesus replied "Love the Lord with all your heart and with all your soul and with all your mind."*

What is your heart's attitude towards God? Do you think of God as a mean judge? Do you think of Him as some unpredictable, whimsical being? Or is He to you like Santa Claus: giving you everything you want as long as you are a good boy or girl? God is good and worthy to be praised and worshipped. He gave us life and all the good things that we have. A constant appreciation of His goodness is the attitude of a true worshipper.

A person who would seek to truly worship God realizes that God is Sovereign and perfect and God all by Himself. He does not need any validation from man to be God. Lack of belief in Him does not take away from His deity, and He does not have to do anything for us and yet, He does. For these reasons, we should be ready to thank and praise Him for the little things, even as we trust Him for bigger things.

David was called a man after God's heart because even though he was weak and imperfect, his attitude towards God was one of reverence and humility. So, as you meditate on the goodness of God, let the attitude of your heart be one of reverence, awe, gratefulness and faith because out of this will flow sincere praise to God.

SCRIPTURE READING: 2 Samuel 22

DOXOLOGY

I love you my Lord, my God, my King. I love you more than anything in heaven or on earth. I worship you heavenly Father with my heart, my mind, my soul, my substance. Everything I am cries out in praise of your glory. I love you because you first loved me and in this you have taught me what love is. You are love and love is you. Jehovah God of agape love, you are worthy of adoration. You are patient, you are kind, you are great and awesome. I praise you Lord of love.

⁓ Day 2 ⁓

PUTTING GOD FIRST

(Exodus 20:3) *You shall have no other gods before me.*

What does this mean? It means regarding God more highly than you regard anyone or anything else: family, career, money, possessions, and friends. It means that if it came to deciding which path to follow, the answer would be to follow God *every time.* Anyone or anything that you place above God automatically takes on the "god" role in your life. You cannot truly worship God or glorify Him when you have an "idol" in your life taking God's rightful place.

Ask yourself these questions: Would I rather follow God's commandment not to steal or help myself to the company's money? Would I rather consistently watch television than consistently fellowship with God? Would I take a job that would compromise my Godly principles? There are probably countless questions such as these that we could ask ourselves.

Consistently putting God first is not easy, neither is it something that you can ever be done with. As long as we are on earth, there will always be the temptation to give God a backseat in our lives. However, as Christians, we have to constantly make the effort to put Him first in our day to day lives; not just on Sunday mornings. As we consciously do this, we will find it easier to get into deeper levels of worship.

SCRIPTURE READING: Exodus 20

DOXOLOGY

Jehovah God, jealous God who will share glory with no other, I bow before you in reverence of your Holy Name. Exalted One, you are number one, no one and no possession can ever take your place in my life. Who is like you Lord? There is none before you, none after You, You are the Alpha and Omega, the Beginning and the End, the First and the Last. I fear you Lord, I honor You, I revere You, Most High; King above kings, God above gods. You are God.

᠍ Day 3 ᠍

BE BORN AGAIN

(Romans 10:10) *For it is with your heart that you believe and are justified, and it is with your mouth that you confess and are saved.*

In order to worship God effectively and be pleasing to Him, you have to be born again. What this means in simple terms is to believe that Jesus Christ came to earth to die for your redemption (from sin, sickness and poverty) and to declare it. Getting born again qualifies you to enter the Kingdom of God. This kingdom is not necessarily a physical kingdom, but a representation of God's way of doing things, God's way of living. It is not something spooky, it is making your peace with God. It is a different perspective of life with God at its center.

If you are not born again yet, give it a thought after you have read the relevant scriptures in this chapter. This is a crucial step for developing a relationship with God and becoming a true worshipper of the Father. You may think about it as you go through the rest of the devotional.

If you decide to make your peace with God, say the simple prayer at the back of this book. Say it with meaning and as you do, the Spirit of God will come into your life, God will cleanse you from all your sins and you will become a child of God with access to the Father.

You now have the power to enter into God's way of doing things including worshipping Him the right way. Now, if you once gave your life over to God through Christ and for various reasons you stopped living a godly lifestyle and let go of the things of God, you can say the prayer at the back of the book and let God restore you into His kingdom. He misses you, He wants you back. God bless you. A few relevant Bible passages are: John 1:12, Romans 8:14, Romans 10, Psalm 51.

SCRIPTURE READING: John 3

DOXOLOGY

Great God Almighty, the One who chose me before I could ever have chosen to serve you, I praise You. You sent Your Son to die for me so I could become Your child. I am ever so grateful for Your redeeming grace in my life. But for Your mercies I would not be alive today. Father of all spirits, thank You for making me spiritually alive in Christ.

↬ Day 4 ↫

GIVING DIRECTLY TO GOD

(Psalm 22:3, KJV) *But thou art holy, O thou that inhabitest the praises of Israel.*

Here is a point to ponder: Praise is the only thing that we give directly to God. Really? What about money? God does not spend it. What about prayer? Well, usually we are praying TO God for ourselves or someone else. What about time? If it is time spent praying, maybe you are doing it more for yourself or your fellow man; if it is time spent in worship, the argument above holds true. What about preaching the gospel, or sharing our faith? We evangelize to help our fellow men not to go to hell.

God neither lives in houses made by men, nor does He need us to feed, clothe or shelter Him! Think about it, you give praise to God and He receives it. This is probably why the Bible talks about God inhabiting the praises of His people. He loves to receive the praise of His children, He delights in it. Do not take this lightly. If you had to present a gift to a king or the president, you would not give a shabby gift, carelessly wrapped, thrown in His face.

You would give something of worth to an earthly king and you would present it with respect and reverence. How often do we sing songs of praise, (either in our personal devotional time or during worship services) while our minds drift off to wonder what is on the lunch menu! As you praise God today, in your thoughts, words, songs, prayers and in just living for his glory; do it with a consciousness that you are truly giving something precious to the One who is the King above all kings.

SCRIPTURE READING: Acts 7: 8-50

DOXOLOGY

I give you Lord my highest praise. You are the one who dwells in the praise of your people. I lift You high, Majestic One, Mighty Man of war. You are the One whose power created all of heaven and all of earth; the planets and the galaxies besides. None can stand before your awesome splendor. You do not live in homes made by men's hands; You do not consume the delectable dishes of man; You do not spend money. Your desire is my praise and I give it to You wholeheartedly. I will praise You forever.

∾ Day 5 ∾

PHD

(Psalm 150:4) *Praise Him with tambourine and dancing; praise Him with the strings and flute.*

Are you wondering what "PHD" is doing in a praise devotional? This title does not stand for Doctor of Philosophy; it stands for Praise Him in Dancing! Yes it does! There is absolutely nothing wrong with dancing to praise God as long as the reason you are dancing is to do just that (praise and worship Him) and not to show off your moves or attract attention.

Dancing is essentially moving to a beat and in the world today dancing takes many forms, not the least being the provocative gyrations seen in clubs and on dance floors.

When done out of a pure heart, dancing to praise God liberates you and can help you express praise to God in ways that mere words sometimes cannot. Dancing is also an expression of joy. Praise is not meant to be funereal.

There are certainly times to be solemn in God's presence. Praise, however is an expression of how much God means to you and there are times when you need to let go, get rambunctious and express out loud the praises in your heart. That's right: "lose it" in His presence; shake off the shackles of "proper behavior"; throw your arms in the air; bust a move and rejoice in the Lord.

SCRIPTURE READING: Psalm 150

DOXOLOGY

I will rejoice in You my Maker, my Father, my Friend; I will rejoice in You. You are great and praiseworthy. I will sing and dance to the glory of Your Name. You have made me so glad, You have turned my tears into laughter. Jesus, Lover of my soul, Prince of peace, Your loving kindness is better than life itself. My kinsman Redeemer who bought me with a price, You are the source and center of my joy. I will dance before You like King David, rejoicing in the glory of Your Name.

⤳ Day 6 ⤳

MUSIC: A TOOL

(**Psalm 66:2**) *Sing to the glory of His Name; make His praise glorious.*

God loves music. How do we know? For one He created it. For another He had an archangel Lucifer dedicated to worshipping Him who later corrupted music when he fell from heaven. Music is an excellent way to worship, although it is not the only way. As a Christian you need to be listening to the music of sound Christian singers whose focus is first and foremost worshipping God.

Listen to praise and worship music as you reflect on God's goodness. Play worship songs at home or in your car. It is amazing how many Christians know who is who in secular hip-hop but have no idea about many Christian singers and artistes.

I dare say that a Christian should listen mostly to Christian music because it feeds your spirit with the praise of God which in turn fills your life with the presence of God.

The presence of God creates an atmosphere of increasing faith and makes room for miracles to flow in your life. Secular music, melodious as it is, will not do this much for you. So, if you have not heard a Christian album lately, go out and buy a CD or download some tracks. You will be glad you did.

SCRIPTURE READING: Psalm 66

DOXOLOGY

I will sing unto You, Lord, a joyful song and praise Your Name because You are good and Your mercy endures everlasting. God, Great God, Light of my life who shines forever bright, You cause darkness to flee. You gave me a song, and I will sing Your praise from now until eternity. If I had a thousand tongues, dialects and languages, I would not be able to describe your glory. You are exalted forever: King immortal, King invincible, King indescribable, Awesome God!

⌒ Day 7 ⌒

MY LIFE SUCKS

(Psalm 103:2) *Praise the Lord, o my soul, and forget not His benefits------*

You may be reading this and thinking, my life is a mess, I have nothing to praise God for. Let me challenge you: you do have something to praise God for and it is just human nature to focus on all that is going wrong instead of even a few things that are going right. When I am in the dumps, I try to remember the smallest thing that I have.

If you are reading this, praise God for your eyesight. If it is being read to you, thank God that you can hear. If you are in the hospital, thank God that you are conscious enough to read. If your marriage is in trouble, praise God that you even have a spouse.

If you are divorced, thank God that you will get a second chance. If you are a busy mother, praise God that you have children. If you have a home to live in, thank God for it. If you have a job, thank God for the opportunity to work.

If you are a pastor, praise God for the call on your life. If you were robbed, thank God that your life was spared. If you are bereaved or grieving, give God praise for the life that your loved one had and thank God for His comfort. My point is, if you look hard enough you will find something praiseworthy in your life and something to give thanks to God for.

In praising Him through the challenges, struggles and pressures of life, you will find that God will bring you to a place of peace and comfort. Apart from that, He will give you wisdom and provide you with solutions that can only be found in His presence. Praise Him in spite of your troubles.

SCRIPTURE READING: Psalm 103

DOXOLOGY

I will bless you Lord in good times and rough times. I will praise and worship you whether I feel like it or not. I will praise You in faith because You are a good God. El-Shaddai, Adonai, You are the Way Maker, the One who causes springs to flow out of deserts. You are the One who can turn mountains to powdery dust and cause the winds to scatter it. You are the heavenly One to whom nothing, nothing, nothing is impossible. Who is like unto You, Shepherd, Savior, King.

⁓ Day 8 ⁓

JOY, JOY, JOY

(Proverbs 29:6) *Evildoers are snared by their own sin, but the righteous shout for joy and are glad.*

There is something about singing that makes you happy. A lifestyle of praise keeps you joyful, and joy in the Lord is the key to maintaining a positive attitude in spite of whatever challenges or struggles you may be faced with. This joy is found in the presence of God and the easiest way to get into His presence and maintain an atmosphere of His presence is by praising Him.

The joy you have is closely connected with your faith in God (people of faith should be joyful, knowing that they have something the world does not have nor can rob them of – a close relationship with God). Since scripture says that without faith, you cannot please God, you would do well to get into the habit of maintaining your joy. Someone once said, "Happiness depends on happenings but joy does not". This means that joy is a deeper inward sensation which does not depend on your circumstances.

A joyful spirit attracts people. If you stay joyful, people will want to know what it is that makes you so happy and in time they will want what you have. Are you feeling sad? Are circumstances getting you down? Switch your focus to God and praise Him. Your joy will return. Make a consistent effort to stay joyful through praise and your life will be ever so colorful, much more attractive, and your faith will rise to new heights.

SCRIPTURE READING: Psalm 16

DOXOLOGY

I will rejoice in You my Lord and King for Your joy is my strength. I will bless you Lord at all times and Your praise will always be on my lips. Everything in me will praise You and boast in Your goodness. I extol You Jehovah Rohi- Lord my shepherd; Jehovah Ezer- Lord my help; Abba Father. You are my joy, You make me glad. Eternal Rock of Ages, the One who was and is and is to come, I shout Hallelujah.

ᨠ Day 9 ᨠ

THE JUST SHALL
LIVE (WORSHIP) BY FAITH

(Philippians 3:3) *For it is we who are the circumcision, we who worship by the Spirit of God, who glory in Christ Jesus, and who put no confidence in the flesh.*

What if you just do not "feel it"? What about those times when you do not feel like praising God, maybe you are just not in an elated "praisy" mood? My answer to that is: do it anyway. The key is to start and the desire will follow the effort. Start with a song that means a lot to you if you are alone trying to worship.

If you are in a congregation, stop, close your eyes and ponder on the meaning of the song/hymn being sung and allow the Holy Spirit to minister to you. God will meet you at your point of need because He is made strong in our weaknesses. If you still do not "feel it" put your trust in the fact that in spite of how you feel God is accepting your worship. As with most other things in life, there are times when we must worship by faith. You do not stop believing in God because you do not see him, and you do not stop believing He is a good God because something went wrong.

Therefore the fact that you do are not in the mood to worship should not make you doubt His presence or doubt your worship.

He accepts your praise, just as He accepts you. Do not put confidence in the flesh i.e. in the physical feeling that comes with worship but put your confidence in the Spirit of God to lift you up. The scripture reading starts with a man lamenting about how God had forgotten him and ends with him rejoicing. He was probably not in the mood to praise God but because of the faith he had in God he praised Him anyway.

SCRIPTURE READING: Psalm 13

DOXOLOGY

Glorious God, my Fortress, my Deliverer, my Guide- I trust in You. I will call upon You in praise, night and day. I will lift Your holy Name higher and higher in exaltation. Righteous One who shines like the morning sun, the One who gives me each breath that I take and every beat that my heart makes; I take delight in offering You praise. Mighty One who parted the red sea, from whom nothing is hidden- I choose to live by faith and worship You in faith. I will praise You and because You have treated me with grace.

ᴄᴐ Day 10 ᴄᴐ

BASED ON HIS WORD

(1 Thessalonians 5:21) *Test everything. Hold on to the good.*

I s your worship based on the Bible, the Word of God? The Bible should be the final authority in a believer's life. Pay close attention to the worship songs you listen to and sing. If they are not based on the word, then they will neither glorify God nor bless you very much. A number of so called praise and worship songs are not praise songs at all; and a good number of "Christian" songs are steeped in unbelief. Here is a checklist to consider in selecting your "Christian" songs:

- Does your Christian song contradict what God's Word says about you? E.g. "I am just a poor sinner". The Bible calls us saints.
- Is your worship song asking for forgiveness for some sin or the other? Well if that is the only theme of the song then it is not a worship song, it may be a song of forgiveness or consecration.
- Does the song you are singing repeatedly beg for something explicitly promised in God's Word? e.g. "Jesus do not pass me by". The Bible says, He will never leave us nor forsake us.

- Does the song talk about how we continuously suffer in this world but will be saved "in the sweet by and by"? Sorry folks, a song about future hope is not a worship song and song about suffering endlessly in this life is not exactly in faith as Jesus came to give us life and life more abundantly. Poor Christians barely making it into heaven does not sound like abundant life to me!
- Does your so called praise song talk endlessly about the devil? e.g. "down, down Satan". A song of worship to God has no mention of the devil in it.

The list is endless but you can probably see what I mean. Test everything including the "Christian" songs and hymns that appeal to your emotions. Ask yourself what the meaning of the song is. Remember God is not glorified merely because a song is slow or because you shed a few tears over an emotionally moving (yet not Word based) song.

SCRIPTURE READING: 1 Thessalonians 5

DOXOLOGY

I give You Lord, Your due praise, based on Your Word. I praise You in the sanctuary. I praise You Lord of all heaven. I praise You Lord for Your mighty acts. I praise You Father according to Your excellent greatness. I praise You my King with songs; I praise You Lord with a dance. Above all sweet Jesus, I will praise You with my life and I will praise You by Your Word. Amen.

᧐ Day 11 ᧐

WALKING IN LOVE

(Matthew 5:23-24) *Therefore, if you are offering your gift at the altar and there remember that your brother has something against you; leave your gift there in front of the altar. First go and be reconciled to your brother; then come and offer your gift.*

One cannot talk about any of the principles of God without talking about love. While this is not a discourse on love per se, it is pertinent to mention that without walking in love towards your fellow man, your praise virtually falls on deaf ears. Your prayers, praises, prophesies, etc are just noise if you harbor hatred, malice and unforgiveness towards your fellow man.

This love speaks of agape-the unconditional love that God has for all of us and expects us to show to our fellow man, Christians and non-Christians alike. This is why Jesus said what He said so explicitly in the verse above. Before you give praise to God, make sure that you are not harboring ill will towards anyone. Grudges and malice hurt the person bearing them.

Did someone do you wrong? Ask for the grace of God to forgive if you are not able to do so in your own strength. Strife is dangerous and as a Christian it should be far from you if you want to make progress in your worship life and in your relationship with God as a whole.

SCRIPTURE READING: 1 Corinthians 13

DOXOLOGY

I love You Lord and I thank You because You love me. You are the Quintessence of love eternal, the never ending fountain of grace, mercy and kindness that never ever ends. Your agape is a love that truly passes understanding. You accept the meekest of lowly hearts and You exalt him beyond his wildest dreams. Your love is comforting, reassuring, a blessing in time of need. Your love is higher than the highest; deeper than the deepest; wider than the widest; bigger than the biggest. Your love for me gives me confidence that all is well and You will never let me go. Thank you for loving me, I will walk in the light of Your love.

༄ Day 12 ༄

IN HIS PRESENCE

(Acts 16:25-26) *About midnight Paul and Silas were praying and singing hymns to God and the other prisoners were
listening to them........*

Praising God does not just give you a good
feeling; it brings the presence of God on the
scene. Let me draw two parallels. In our Old
Testament scripture reading we see Daniel praying for
a solution which eventually takes 21 days to arrive. In
our New Testament scripture reading, Paul and Silas
sang praises unto God and instantly, God manifested
His presence in their midst.

Praise brings God Himself on the scene. Could it be
that if Daniel had a revelation about praise, his story
would have been different? When you praise God either alone or in a gathering of believers, He shows
up. God finds sincere praise irresistible. This is why
He God called David, a man without a stellar record,
a man after His heart. What a great way to enjoy His
presence, by opening your heart and worshipping the
Most High God.

Also as I mentioned in a previous chapter, when God comes on the scene, He brings wisdom, solutions, strength, peace and miracles.

Decide to start your prayer with worship either in words, in the Spirit, or in songs. Adopting a lifestyle of worship makes your prayer life to be less of a struggle. When you feel God is actually nearby, and listening to you, it is easier to believe Him for answers. Another helpful tip: have a session of worship before you read your Bible and you will find greater clarity of the Word, just from being surrounded by the presence of God.

SCRIPTURE READINGS: Acts 16:17-25; Daniel 10:12-14

DOXOLOGY

Most High God, Omnipresent King of glory, Father, Son, Holy Spirit I honor You. I choose to make praising You my priority. I give myself over completely to the praise and glory of Your Name. Great I Am that I Am, worthy are you. In Your presence mountains melt like wax; Your enemies are scattered; the earth shakes and trembles; problems disappear; chains of oppression are broken asunder. Your bearing is awesome, so magnificent, so indescribable. Praise to You Lord.

Ᏼ Day 13 Ᏼ

WORSHIP...IN OTHER TONGUES

(1 Corinthians 14:2) *For anyone who speaks in a tongue does not speak to men but to God. Indeed, no one understands him; he utters mysteries in his spirit.*

Apart from songs of praise, worshipping God in other tongues is a surefire way to get into deeper realms of worship. This is true worship in the Spirit because you are telling God exactly what He wants to hear! Think about it.

The Holy Spirit who helps us speak the heavenly language (i.e. speak in tongues) is the third person of the trinity. So what better way to worship God than by His own Spirit? The same way you pray and sing with your understanding, you can pray and sing by the inspiration of the Holy Spirit.

It may seem strange if you are not used to it but if you keep at it, you will find your life enriched as you begin to enter into depths of worship and depths of God's presence.

You may find yourself automatically bursting out in tongues or singing in the spirit when your heart is so full with worshipping God that you cannot express yourself in your understanding. Just yield to the Spirit of God and your life will not remain the same.

SCRIPTURE READING: 1 Corinthians 14

DOXOLOGY

Revealer of secrets, Mighty, and Mysterious One; who on earth can compare to you? Who is worthy of praise like You are? Oh Lord of mercy and compassion, who hears me when I call; I worship You this day in spirit and in truth. I choose now to enter into a new realm of worship in the Spirit. I will sing new songs and psalms to praise you, for there is no praise, no worship, no honor, nor any rejoicing too great for you, King of glory. Thank You Greater One, Thank You for leading me in true exaltation of your Name.

❧ Day 14 ❧

TITHING WITH THE RIGHT ATTITUDE

(Matthew 23:23) *Woe to you, teachers of the law and Pharisees, you hypocrites! You give a tenth of your spices—mint, dill and cumin. But you have neglected the more important matters of the law—justice, mercy and faithfulness. You should have practiced the latter, without neglecting the former.*

This chapter is not really about tithing. I once heard a preacher say, "Give God 10% of your income and 100% of your heart". How often do we see Christians who are faithful tithers but have not truly given God first place in their hearts? To these brothers and sisters, tithing has become a religious ritual and lost its true meaning.

What glory do you give to God if you put 10% of your income in the offering box but still harbor malice and unforgiveness and disobey the commandments of God? God cannot be bribed with money. He does not need it as He looks first at the heart. Your life needs to be totally turned over to God, making Him the centre of your life, putting Him first in all things.

Then and only then will your offerings be acceptable to God. Do not stop paying your tithes and giving your offerings unto God. Present it to Him with a heart of worship and not as a ritual or a bribe. At the end of the age when your works are tested by God for your motives, will you pass the test or will your works be burned in the fire?

SCRIPTURE READING: 1 Corinthians 3:10-15

DOXOLOGY

Lord I give You my heart, my spirit, soul and body. I present myself wholly to You, a living sacrifice, acceptable for my masters use. All I am and all I have is Yours. You are not a man that can be mocked. You are the One who searches the deep things of the heart. You speak in a still small voice, yet You speak with the voice of a torrent. You are so mighty yet You have given me significance. I give it all to You, all seeing, all knowing, all wise, all powerful God.

᎒ Day 15 ᎒

ACKNOWLEDGE
THE POWER

(**Ephesians 1:19**)...*and His incomparably great power for us who believe.*

Worship acknowledges God as THE SU-PREME BEING. It realizes that God has and is the ultimate power and glory and might. Whenever you bow your head to worship God, meditate on the fact that he is awesome, He is God, and not to be trifled with.

Remember that He created the whole world out of nothing and should He choose to, He can send His created world back into nothingness! God has the power to transform a situation in an instant and the power to perform extraordinary feats (we call these miracles).

If you are getting "used to" God, a little blasé or familiar with Him, open your Bible and read about, the plagues, read the Psalms, read about all the miracles of Jesus and the Acts of the Apostles.

Ask God to reveal Himself to you in a new way. Meditate on scriptures that talk about the power and the majesty of God. As you acknowledge the power of God, remember that this same power, the power that raised Christ from the dead is at work in you and at your disposal, always there for you to call upon when you need it.

Think about this as you go through your day to day life; and as you worship and praise Him. Renew your awareness of the great and awesome power of God. You will begin to see more of the manifestations of His might in your life.

SCRIPTURE READING: Ephesians 1:15-23

DOXOLOGY

Rock of Ages, God of might, the One who leads His warriors in victory, time and time again. God of greatness, Ruler of heaven whose footstool is earth; who has founded the heavens and earth by changeless decrees; who establishes His covenant forever. You hold the stars in the firmament and keep the planets in orbit. Ancient of ancients, yet You never age; Holiest of holy ones; Righteous Judge of all men, there is none who can question or contest Your Word. I give You praise.

∽ Day 16 ∽

RENEW YOUR MIND...
PROBLEM SOLVED

(Romans 12:2a) *Do not conform any longer to this world but be transformed by the renewing of your mind.*

When you renew your mind by meditating on God's Word concerning His greatness, you automatically begin to marvel at that greatness. As you worship Him more and more in your daily life, there comes a point where your problems, challenges and issues shrink in comparison to God's power and greatness. When that happens, your faith in God is strengthened and your capacity to believe Him for solutions is expanded.

Here is an analogy: Let us suppose there was a neighborhood bully who looked big and menacing because he was ten years old and you were four. By mere size and age, he was obviously bigger than you were. Every time you passed by his house, he ran out to hit you on the head and pushed you over. One day you told your dad and he offered to watch out for you as you passed the bully's home.

The next day you walked by with confidence knowing that your dad had your back. The bully came out and just as he started to run at you, you pointed towards your dad who was standing up the street. Suddenly, the "big" bully did not look so big anymore because your dad was standing by.

Out of the blue, the bully changed his mind, seeing your dad standing there; he did not want to take him on. So it is when you focus on the power of God instead of the size of your problems. They lose their power over us as faith is generated in our hearts.

SCRIPTURE READING: Psalm 18

DOXOLOGY

You are a wondrous God, great in power, bigger far than any mountain I can or cannot see. I extol You. Fearful One, High and Mighty; Holy and Anointed; Gracious and Merciful; Risen and Exalted; Grand and Glorious; I raise You to the highest place above all else. Mighty Warrior with armor of light who drives away darkness so that it never returns. You are greater, much greater than any problem that may present itself to me. I magnify You, You are God. Hallelujah.

⟟ Day 17 ⟟

ENTER BOLDLY

(Hebrews 4:16) *Let us therefore approach the throne of grace with confidence, so that we may receive mercy and find grace to help us in time of need.*

How do you approach God in the place of praise and worship? We are not meant to come before God cringing in fear of a God of whim and caprice; neither are we to come with feelings of inferiority, crushed under the weight of guilt, shame and defeat.

We are to approach God confidently (not arrogantly) according to the scripture above, knowing well that we will receive grace, mercy and help. On the flip side, we are not to come to God in prayer with a wish list of all our needs and wants with no real desire to fellowship with our Father.

What normal son of a normal father goes up to him and says; "Daddy, I am not worthy to be called your child......"? Dad would think his loving son had gone round the bend! Or what normal child has no conversation with his or her father except to recite a list of what he or she wants? So, remember whether you are worshiping alone or in a congregation, go into His presence with reverence, boldness and the joy that comes with being a child of God.

SCRIPTURE READING: Hebrews 4

DOXOLOGY

King of heaven, Creator of earth, the One who wears a crown of glory and ever increases in glory; I come boldly before your throne of grace to fellowship and to enjoy your presence. Eternal Lord of Lords, I just want to be close to You, To know You more, to see you more clearly. God of gods, Light of light, Father of the father less; husband to the widow, I cherish You. Thank you for granting grace to come before You.

ᘐ Day 18 ᘐ

DRIVING OUT THE ENEMY

(2 Chronicles 20:17) *You will not have to fight this battle. Take up your positions; stand firm and see the deliverance that the Lord will give you, O Judah and Jerusalem. Do not be afraid, do not be discouraged. Go out and face them tomorrow and the Lord will be with you.*

Today we see Jehoshaphat defeating the armies that came against him just by praising the Lord. We see something similar in the book of Joshua where the wall of Jericho came down when God commanded the people to shout.

The same thing can happen in our lives when we declare the goodness of God over our lives *at his instruction*. Note that all these men of God were warriors who had prepared for war to the best of their ability. They were not just loafing around, being lazy, and then asking God to bail them out.

God knew that they would need His power to defeat the armies and He provided it by getting the people to praise Him and thus focus on His power. Nothing brings His presence like praise and once they started

41

to praise God, His miraculous power was manifested, putting the enemies to flight. Child of God, when you have prayed, you have believed and in God's wisdom you have done all that you know to do, open your mouth and let your praise go up to heaven.

There is a mystery about praise such that when you give God praise in the midst of a trying situation, He shows up and shows up in a big way. So get noisy and increase the intensity of your praise!

SCRIPTURE READING: 2 Chronicles 20:1-30

DOXOLOGY

Master of the universe, Conqueror of a thousand armies, the One who champions the lost causes and raises champions out of them. Thank You for the victory that comes with praising You. One with You is truly the majority. I will praise You when I face challenges for there is none who gives victory so completely. Powerful Warrior, great in battle; Jehovah Sabbaoth, Lord of hosts, I am an overcomer because I am a praiser. I stand in awe of You.

೨ Day 19 ೨

MOTIVES

(1 John 5:3) *This is love for God: to obey His commands. And His commands are not burdensome.*

Why worship God anyway? Our worship of God should be because we love God, not just another religious exercise ("oh it's just something we do"). Neither should it be done just so you can receive from God. Yes you will receive from God many blessings when you worship and praise Him, but that should not be your motive for praising Him.

The reason to praise God should be because you love Him and want to express the love in your heart towards Him. Remember that God sees into your heart and knows your motives anyway, and to love God is to obey Him. Are you having problems getting your heart back on the right track?

Think about when you first gave your heart to Jesus. Stay focused on His word and strives to obey his commands. Meditate on His love for you and remember why you got born again.

Let the love of God come alive within you and give God the worship He deserves from a pure heart.

SCRIPTURE READING: 1 John 4:7-19

DOXOLOGY

I worship You O Lord for whom You are , not only for Your awesome works. I love You; my heart, my mind, my eyes are all fixed on You as I come before You in worship this day. I will bless You all the time, day and night: Your praise and exaltation will always be on my lips. Elohim, Triune Being, Transcendent One to whom all is bare and plain before Your all-seeing eye and all knowing wisdom, You are truly awesome. I will praise You with a pure heart and holy hands.

☙ Day 20 ❧

IT IS NOT ABOUT YOU

(John 4:23) *Yet a time is coming and has now come when true worshippers will worship the Father in spirit and in truth for they are the kind of worshippers the Father seeks.*

There is a popular Christian chorus that starts with the words, "I forget about myself and concentrate on you to worship you". Worship is about you presenting your life as a living sacrifice to Him. Often I have heard Christians say things like, "I did not really enjoy the praise songs today" or, "I did not 'flow' with the worship songs"; or even "I do not like the worship leader"! Guess what?

Worship is not for you to enjoy, it is for God to enjoy. It is never about the song, it is about what is in your heart. It is not about the instruments (or lack of thereof) or the musical technology or your favorite worship leader.

It is however, about adoring God, with your words, in your singing, in your dancing, in your attitude and in your life. As the aforementioned song says, forget about you because it is not about you.

45

Let God Himself be the focus of your praise and worship, so that whatever the circumstances, you are worshipping God and not indulging in a feel-good emotional session.

SCRIPTURE READING: Psalm 24

DOXOLOGY

It's all about You Lord. My praise and worship is all about You. You reign and rule on high in splendor, in righteousness, in glory, in power, in mercy, in judgment and in love. I exalt You Lord above everything vying for my attention. You are worthy of the highest place. Take all my praise today, El-Elyon-Most High God; the One who is there and ever faithful. Jehovah Shamma. I worship and adore You Holy One of Israel because it is all about You!

⁐ Day 21 ⁐

GET EXCITED ABOUT GOD

(Revelation 2:4) *Yet I hold this against you. You have forsaken your first love.*

If you are a parent you would no doubt have had that warm feeling you get when your children are excited to see you. My daughter greets me with unparalleled enthusiasm every time I walk through the door and especially if I have had a rough day, this uplifts my spirits every time.

You are made in the image of God, so can you imagine what joy it would bring to His heart if you were always excited about Him in prayer, praise, and attending local assembly services.

Unfortunately with Christians, this is not always the case. Too often we become familiar with God, so to speak. We get used to praying, singing, going "to church", giving offerings etc so much that after a while it all becomes a drag. We lose our zeal and passion for the things of God to the point that we even stop doing them! This should not be the case.

When you praise or worship God, it gladdens His heart. When you do so with the fervor and excitement of a two year old child; greeting her parents for the umpteenth time, it brings Him joy.

Return to your first love: that initial excitement that you had when you first came in contact with the kingdom of God, that initial contact that brought out the child-like faith and zeal in you. Return to doing those things you used to do and stir up your passion for Him once again.

SCRIPTURE READING: Revelation 2:1-8

DOXOLOGY

Hallelujah! Glory to Your Name! Your mercies are new everyday so I will lift my heart to You and lift my voice to shout and sing Your praise. Oh God! My soul will boast of Your goodness, night and day. I am ever so grateful for Your unending grace and Your unfailing love. I will not become blasé about Your patience and unending kindness. God, You are so good to me. Adonai, You are forever. You are the reason that I am and the pillar that holds my life. Glory to Your Name!

❦ Day 22 ❦

PRACTICING HIS PRESENCE

(1 Thessalonians 5:17, KJV) *Pray without ceasing.*

Paul talks about praying without ceasing. I do not believe that this means walking around all day whispering your prayers and doing nothing else. It is my belief that this means being conscious of God's presence and turning your mind to Him every now and then. It means listening for His voice in all situations and being ready to obey.

"Practicing His presence" means that you are in communication with God throughout the day. It means your worship of God is not relegated only to your morning devotional sessions and Sunday services. What does this have to do with praising God?

The consciousness of God's presence at all times brings you closer to Him and enables you to praise and communicate with Him more effectively and freely than sporadic praise and worship. Am I saying abandon regular times of fellowship and worship or stop gathering with believers for Sunday worship? NO!

What I am saying is that, in addition to those set times, it is important to cultivate the habit of practicing His presence. Your relationship with God will be enriched through this closer fellowship that you will enjoy with Him.

SCRIPTURE READING: Psalm 16

DOXOLOGY

Good Shepherd who causes me not to lack- I choose Your presence, I choose to live in Your presence every moment of every day. In You presence there is life, joy, peace, blessing, and pleasures forever and ever. In Your presence there is security and all I would ever need. Great Comforter, Helper, Succour, Strength, I will practice Your presence. Draw me close to You according to Your Word. I know You will never let me go. Savior, Master, Redeemer, my Best Friend, outside You, there is no place to go. Praise the Lord!

～ Day 23 ～

ALTOGETHER NOW

(Psalm 149:1) *Praise the Lord. Sing to the Lord a new song, His praise in the assembly of the saints.*

This chapter is about how to worship God during a worship service and how to get the best out of corporate worship. First, on your way to the gathering, prepare yourself by trying to relax and free your mind from the mental stresses of everyday life. Meditate on a scripture or two that speak about the specific attributes of God. Expect that you are going to have a wonderful time in His presence. If you have un-confessed sins, repent of them *before the service*.

First and foremost, when the praise and worship starts, focus on God, and not on the choir leader's clothes or how they are not doing it right. Close your eyes if that is what it takes to stay focused. Secondly, do not let yourself get distracted and also try not to distract others by waving to your friends, chewing gum loudly, or trying to sing above the choir leader's voice. Thirdly, praise God from your heart and expect God to speak to your heart too. Expect to hear from Him.

Last but not least, try your best to follow instructions from the pulpit. For instance: "can we kneel to sing this hymn", or "lift up your hands and praise the Lord" or "shout hallelujah", - to mention a few. This will help you get into the "vibe" and not feel like an outsider.

If the style of worship is new to you, try not to get caught up with looking skeptically at your fellow worshippers. God is not worried about the style of worship so you should not be. Just focus on God, refuse distractions and enjoy His presence.

SCRIPTURE READING: Psalm 149

DOXOLOGY

I praise You Lord! I praise You with all the saints who daily praise Your Name. I praise You with all the angels and hosts of heaven. I praise You with the sun, moon and stars so bright. I praise You, together with the heavens that You made. You are good, upright and unquestionable. You are exalted above all creation. The world will hear Your praise from my lips. All encompassing God in whom all things exist, I render due praise to You.

ᥟ Day 24 ᥟ

HAVE A THEME

(**Psalm 45:1**) *My heart is stirred by a noble theme as I recite my verses for the king; my tongue is the pen of a skillful writer.*

Here is a helpful tip. Something I have found which helped me in my years as a worship leader and still helps me in my personal worship time is to have a theme for worship. What I mean is focusing on a certain aspect or quality of God during a worship session.

Let us say for example that you want to focus on the faithfulness of God. You would perhaps initially read some scriptures that talk about God's faithfulness. If you were leading a worship session, you could share the relevant Bible verses with the congregation.

Using the Word as a focus for worship is not only pleasing to God but also helps you to renew your mind along the lines of your theme. Examples of other themes are His holiness, His greatness, His majesty, His love, His wisdom, His power, etc. This applies more to leaders of worship: It helps to get the congregation ready for the preacher's sermon if praise and worship songs along the lines of the sermon for the day are sung. This sort of "connected worship" creates an atmosphere of faith and gets people spiritually and mentally ready for the sermon. This is one of the many ways believers benefit from worshipping God.

SCRIPTURE READING: Psalm 136

DOXOLOGY

I praise You Heavenly Father because you are praiseworthy. I worship You God of all. You are the One from whom all life flows and the one from whom all blessings come. I adore You. You are the quintessence of love everlasting; the never ending fountain of wisdom and truth. You of all being are the greatest yet you grant to me the privilege of being Your child. You made me in Your image to bring glory to Your Name. Who is like You? None! Alpha and Omega, the beginning and the End- I stand forever in awe of You.

◌ Day 25 ◌

DISCERN HIS WILL

(Romans 12:2, ISV) *Do not be conformed to this world, but continually be transformed by the renewing of your minds so that you may be able to determine what God's will is—what is proper pleasing, and perfect.*

What does God want me to do? Whether you are praising God in your devotional session or leading a worship session, it is important to discern the will of God for the moment. Search your heart after you get quiet in His presence and ask yourself, "How does God want me to praise Him?"

This may be easy in a setting of a private worship session but when leading a congregation, you have to be prepared to hear and obey the voice of God and lead people in the same direction.

I have been in worship services where the Spirit of God was leading people just to kneel silently in His presence and worship Him. At certain times God may want you to sing certain songs or depart from your usual style of worship.

This is where as a worship leader, you may need to use scripture to get everyone in one accord especially if people are used to doing things in a certain way. In a personal worship session God may be asking you to worship in a different way from what you are used to. Do not panic. Follow the Spirit of God and you will be blessed.

Remember, God is trying to bless you, not make you feel uncomfortable. Also remember that He will not lead you outside of His Word. Let your praise and worship of Him go to another level by just getting quiet in His presence and following His leading.

SCRIPTURE READING: Joshua 6

DOXOLOGY

Lord of heaven, I will worship you according to Your will and Your way, not mine; I will follow where You lead in worship. Lord of light, open the eyes of my heart, so I can see what You want me to see in the place of worship. *Waymaker*, guide my path as I seek greater depths of fellowship with You. Faithful God, Righteous Father, Holy One of Israel; Strong Tower for the upright; my meat is to do Your will in all things, even worship. Praise be to You oh God!

ᑌᦓ Day 26 ᑐᦓ

WAYS TO PRAISE

(Hebrews 13:15) *Through Jesus, therefore, let us continually offer to God a sacrifice of praise—the fruit of lips that confess his name.*

There are many ways of expressing praise to God. Here is a list that is not exhaustive but it lists some biblical ways of praising God. Some of these have already been dealt with in detail in previous chapters.

1. Singing: When we talk about praise and worship, this is what usually comes to mind (Psalm 47:6).
2. Clapping: You can clap in praise to God with or without music or singing (Psalm 47:1).
3. Shouting: Shouting in praise is scriptural too! In Hebrew this is called *"Shabach"* (Zephaniah 3:14). The Hebrew word *"Tehillah"* is a word which denotes a combination of shouting, singing, clapping and rejoicing.
4. Playing instruments: You can play an instrument to praise God. The Hebrew word for this is *"Zamar"* (Psalm 150).
5. Dancing: This is addressed in a previous chapter. It is called *"Hallel"* in Hebrew and dancing does not always have to be to music or a beat.

You can praise God in a dance all on its own.

6. Tongues: It is scriptural, hence spiritual to praise God in other tongues. You can sing in tongues also (1 Corinthians 14:15).

7. Lifting hands: Called *"Yadah"* in Hebrew. This is lifting your hands in submission and reverence to God (Psalm 134:2).

8. Bowing down: To bow down and worship God is to express awe at His majesty. This is *"Barouch"* in Hebrew (Psalm 95:6).

9. Solemn silence: There are times to be quiet in God's presence and honor Him with solemn silence. It is during these times that God speaks to you. While praise and worship is usually an outward expression of your love for God, there are times when God wants you to be quiet and just bask in His presence (Psalm 46:10).

SCRIPTUE READING: Psalm 138

DOXOLOGY

I extol You, Amazing God. I will praise You in every way I can for You are glorious. You shine brighter than the morning sun. Keeper of eternal covenants, the great I am, the One with the most excellent Name, Redeemer of captive souls; most marvelous, most wonderful, indescribably beautiful, with unparalleled glory. I adore You. I raise Your praise. I will sing shout, clap, dance and rejoice because You deserve it all.

∾ Day 27 ∾

CONSISTENCY IN WORSHIP

(Ephesians 5:20, ISV) *You will consistently give thanks to God for everything in the Name of our Lord Jesus the Messiah.*

I once heard a preacher say, "In consistency lies the power". Whatever you do consistently becomes a habit and a habit is something that you do consistently. In order to develop a lifestyle of worship, it is a good idea to spend time worshipping God daily for a consistent amount of time.

This will help you get closer to God as well as make it easier and easier to cultivate an atmosphere of worship. At first, you may need to start small so that you are not overwhelmed. Start with fifteen to twenty minutes at a go.

As time goes by and you really get into it, you will find yourself unconsciously spending more and more time in God's presence. The best time to set apart for worship is probably early in the morning when your mind is clearer. For some people night time might be better.

Due to work schedules, you might not be able to worship at the same time each day. It is however better to try to attain a goal of daily worship and fall short, than not to try at all. Ask the Holy Spirit for wisdom in managing your time so that you can spend more time with your Father. It may mean giving up some television viewing or newspaper reading time but it will be well worth it.

SCRIPTURE READING: Ephesians 5:15-21

DOXOLOGY

I choose You Lord. I choose You above everything else. I choose to give You quality time and quality praise. Earnestly, daily, I will seek Your face and seek Your will. My time is in Your hands Lord, please guide me in its use. Dearest Daddy, one day with You is better than a thousand days anywhere else. I love You. Solid Rock of Ages on which I stand; lion of the Tribe of Judah; Lover of my Soul; Mover of the immovable; Shaker of the unshakeable, I bow in your presence and revere You.

⤳ Day 28 ⤳

EXPECT OPPOSITION

(1 Peter 5:8) *Be self-controlled and alert. Your enemy the devil prowls around like a roaring lion looking for someone to devour.*

If you are going to do anything worthwhile for God, including worshipping and living a life of worship, it is pertinent to realize that the devil is going to fight you tooth and nail to keep you from doing so. The Bible says we are not to be ignorant of the wiles of the enemy. I am not one of those people who see a demon lurking behind every shrub, but neither am I blasé about the fact that the devil does not want me praising God because the more I praise Him, the less the devil's works are able to affect me.

One of the things the devil does is to try to make you forget whatever new things you learn about God. You need to make it a point to keep your focus on God's Word by making an effort to stay in prayer and the Word daily. Another tactic of his is to discourage you by making you feel you can never attain heights of worship and that you will always be mediocre.

To this the Bible says, "I can do all things through Christ who strengthens me." Another trick that works very well against believers is being too busy. You may even be busy doing "church things", at the expense of seeking the real thing, the kingdom of God! Remember, do not get so focused on working for God that you forget God Himself.

Please do not get too busy to spend time with God. Make it a priority. Above all else remember to rely on God. You have the victory that overcomes, which is your faith. God is there to help you, if you try to get ahead in the area of worship and you do not succeed at first, do not give up. You will only make your adversary happy by giving up.

SCRIPTURE READING: 1 Peter 5

DOXOLOGY

I will live for You Lord. I will live the life of worship that You want me to live. Divine Enabler, my heart is always towards You, to love You, obey You and consistently worship You. Your power is greater than what the adversary may bring. Your love is all encompassing, bringing me closer to You. I have faith in You, faithful one. I choose to serve You faithfully and I will resist and denounce the enemy. Restorer, Rewarder, God of manifold blessing - I will live for You.

ᶜ⁹ Day 29 ᶜ⁹

CONFESS YOUR SINS

(Isaiah 43:25) *I, even I, am He who blots out your transgressions for My own sake and remembers your sins no more.*

Un-confessed, un-repented sin in the life of a Christian hinders your ability to live a life of worship. If you commit a sin, confess and repent of it immediately, so that you do not come into condemnation. Sin robs you of your confidence to come before God because His presence is Holy and He cannot stand sin.

Remember, it is not God who condemns you, but the enemy. The devil is called the accuser of the brethren and will always come to remind you of how you sinned; how you cannot go into the presence of God, and how your praise will never be acceptable before the Lord.

The Holy Spirit will convict you of sin and when he does, confess it there and then. Afterwards, move on, because the Bible says He will not even remember our sins!

Additionally, ask for God's strength to keep you from falling into temptation. As you worship God today, make up your mind that you will not allow un-confessed sin to hinder your fellowship with the Father.

SCRIPTURE READING: Psalm 25

DOXOLOGY

Father of lights, in whom there is no variation nor shadow of turning, hallowed be Your Name. How great You are Lord, You blot out sins and never remember them again. Thank You, Merciful King for I know that there is no sin too big for You to forgive. Cleanser and Restorer, Baptizer in the Holy Ghost; the One who saves and saves completely. Thank You Jesus who gave all to save me, there is nothing, no one that I love more than I love you. Praise to You Lord!

⁀ Day 30 ⁀

HUMBLE YOURSELF

(James 4:10) *Humble yourselves before the Lord and He will lift You up.*

The words humble and humility are very commonly misunderstood. In religion today, they are taken to mean a state of self-deprecation, self-degradation and not realizing your own worth. Bible humility is not making yourself into nothing, it is realizing that without God you are nothing and you cannot be everything you are meant to be.

Humility in Christ is recognizing that your sufficiency is not in yourself but in the One who made you and knows everything about you. True worshippers are humble people because to genuflect and worship something or someone you MUST acknowledge the fact that, that thing or being is of a higher status than you are.

As Christians we are also warned about the dangers of pride. All our accomplishments, knowledge, spirituality, etc are nothing before the King of your life who gave you the very breath that you take.

Every good thing that you have has been given to you by God. Remember that God resists the proud but gives grace to the humble.

SCRIPTURE READING: Philippians 3:1-16

DOXOLOGY

Consuming fire! I humble myself under Your mighty hand, I know that You will exalt me in due time, in Your time. Your Excellency! I bow before You in true humility of heart and mind. Ever loving God, the One who was, and is, and is to come; the One who exists outside of time, forever and throughout eternity, You are truly marvelous. Thank You Jesus because there is no me without You Lord. You made me what I am and gave me all I have. Thank You for everything You have done for me. I will praise your Name today, tomorrow, and forever more.

∽ Day 31 ∽

NAMES OF GOD

(Psalm 8:1) *LORD, our Lord, how majestic is your* **name** *in all the earth! You have set your glory above the heavens.* (Emphasis mine)

As you worship God today, meditate on the many different Names of God and allow the Holy Spirit to cause a revelation of the Names to truly come alive in your heart. This list is by no means exhaustive but it does give a picture of the God that we serve and the many reasons to praise and worship Him.

- El: God (Genesis 7:1)
- Elohim: God the Creator, Preserver, Transcendent, Mighty and Strong-Genesis 17:7 (used 2,570 times in the Old Testament)
- El-Elyon: Most High God (Daniel 5:18)
- El Roi: The Lord who sees (Genesis 16:13)
- El-Shaddai: God All Sufficient (Genesis 17:1, 22)
- Adonai: Lord (Psalm 114:7)
- Jehovah: LORD (Genesis 2:4)
- Jehovah Jireh: The Lord will provide (Gen 22:14)
- Jehovah Rapha: The Lord our healer (Exodus 15:22-26)

- Jehovah Nissi: The Lord our banner (Exodus 17:15)
- Jehovah Mekeddeshem: The Lord who sanctifies (Leviticus 20:8)
- Jehovah Shalom: The Lord our peace (Judges 6:24)
- Jehovah Tsidkenu: The Lord our righteousness (Jeremiah 23:5-6)
- Jehovah Rohi: The Lord our Shepherd (Psalm 23)
- Jehovah Shamma: The Lord is there (Ezekiel 48:35)
- Jehovah Sabaoth: The Lord of hosts (Isaiah 47:4)
- Jehovah Ezer: The Lord our help (Psalm 121, Psalm 33:20)
- Alpha and Omega: The beginning and the ending (Revelation 1:8)
- Abba: Father (Galatians 4:6); Almighty (2 Corinthians 6:18); I AM (Exodus 3:14)
- Christ: The Anointed one (Matthew 16:16); Jesus: Savior (2 Peter 3:18); King of Kings, Lord of Lords (1 Timothy 6:15); The God of heaven (Psalm 136:26); Prince of Peace (Isaiah 9:6); Rock of Ages (Isaiah 26:4); Lion of the tribe of Judah (Revelation 5:5)

SCRIPTURE READING: Psalm 8

DOXOLOGY

Psalm 8 - O Lord, our Lord, how majestic is Your Name in all the earth. You have set Your glory above the heavens. From the lips of children and infants You have ordained praise because of Your enemies, to silence the foe and the avenger. When I consider Your heavens, the works of Your fingers, the moon and the stars, which You have set in place, what is man that You are mindful of him, and the son of man that You care for him? You made him a little lower than heavenly beings and crowned him with glory and honor. You made him ruler over the works of Your hands; You put everything under his feet: all flocks and herds and the beasts of the field, the birds of the air, and the fish of the sea, all that swim the paths of the seas. Oh Lord, our Lord, how majestic is Your Name in all the earth!

TIPS FOR
WORSHIP LEADERS

I was a worship leader for a few years, it was not for
very long and I know still have a lot to learn about
leading worship. There are some things I did learn,
sometimes through my own mistakes, learning what
not to do. These tips are not only for choir leaders or
music directors but anyone who would lead a group
in worship at anytime.

1. **Be a closet worshipper:** You have to spend time
    in God's presence just worshipping Him if you are
    going to be an effective worship leader. Do not
    rely solely on externals e.g. your charisma or your
    voice. Spending longer periods of time in worship
    helps to maintain the anointing upon your life.
2. **Practice:** Do not rely on "moving with the Sprit"
    only. Yes, move with the Spirit but do not ne-
    glect the finer points of leading worship i.e. Vari-
    ous songs, stage presence, voice training, etc.
3. **Pray:** If no one else in The Church prays, the
    worship leader MUST be prayerful. Your prayer
    life cannot be toyed with as you cannot afford
    to lose the anointing that God has placed upon
    your life or upon your office as a choir leader.
4. **Sing the melody, not the harmony:** When
    you lead worship, sing only the melody of the
    song. You may of course adlib in order to add
    flavor to your singing, however, consistently
    harmonizing is not excellent worship leading.

In the same vein, if backup leaders are present, they should not skip between parts (e.g. alto to soprano), neither should they adlib.

5. **Be sensitive to God's voice and be ready to obey:** God may want to take the worship session in another direction different from what you have rehearsed. Go with the flow of the Spirit of God (see Discern His Will in Day 25).

6. **Open your eyes:** As a worship leader you are meant to see the congregation. You are leading them into God's presence and if you cannot see what people are doing , there is no way of knowing if people are getting the best of God's presence or not. Another thing is that your closed eyes can act as a curtain preventing people from connecting with what you are connecting with. For a worship leader, this is not your personal time with God. You had that at home (hopefully). This is the time for you to show others the way.

7. **Be up to date with songs:** The fact that you love "Holy, holy, holy" and you enjoy singing it in your personal devotion time does not mean that you should sing it while leading worship. Know your congregation, do your research, get fresh anointing and keep in step with the times.

8. **Be confident:** God has not given you a spirit of timidity but of love, power and a sound mind. Stage presence can be learned. When you pick up a microphone to lead worship, you have the backing of heaven so do not be shy. God placed you there for a reason, so go in the confidence, trusting in the anointing upon your life.

FINAL DOXOLOGY

I praise you Heavenly Father because You are worthy of praise. I worship You because You are God of heaven and earth. You are the Creator of all things, seen and unseen. You are the Master of the universe. You are the One from whom all life flows and from whom all blessings come. I adore you, Lord. You are the quintessence of love everlasting; the never ending fount of life eternal.

You of all beings are the greatest yet You grant me the privilege of being your child. You made me in Your image to bring glory to Your Name. I worship You, King of kings. You are above all else; for Your throne is in heaven and the earth is Your foot stool. Who is like You? Who can compare to Your matchless worth? Who can stand as an equal beside You or before You? You are the Alpha and Omega, the First and the Last, the Beginning, and the End.

Before time was, You were because You created time and it is subject to You. I stand in awe of you, Lord. Lord you are my Father, Friend, Comforter, Savior, Provider, Redeemer, Supporter, Defender, Shield and ever present Help. I commit myself to seeking a deeper relationship with you through praise and worship. I decide to live a life that brings glory to your Name. I love You, Lord. In Jesus Name, Amen.

PRAYER TO RECEIVE SALVATION

In order to start a productive relationship with God, you must surrender your life to the Lordship of Jesus Christ. If you have not accepted Jesus Christ as your Lord and Savior, I encourage you to pray the following prayer aloud in order to receive your salvation

Dear God, I come to you believing that Jesus died on the cross and was raised from the dead to save my soul. I ask you to come into my heart and change me from within enabling me to enter into Your way of living. I confess with my mouth that I believe Jesus died for me and I now receive your gift of salvation. I am now born again. I confess that Jesus Christ is the Son of God and He is now the Lord of my life. Amen.

This is the wisest decision you have ever made. Please, do not look back and endeavor to look for a Bible-believing church where the unadulterated Word of God is being preached and begin to worship there regularly. Buy a Bible and study it daily.

Always ask the Holy Spirit to teach you His word before you study. Welcome to the kingdom of light. May the Lord God bless and uphold you in Jesus mighty name. I am waiting to hear from you. You can contact me through my address toward the end of the book.

ABOUT THE AUTHOR

Adeshola Ezeokoli has served the body of Christ in various capacities ministering to the people of God. She has served church as worship leader, prayer leader, usher, editor.

She is currently the head of the publications department at KingsWord International Church, Chicago. She is married with two children and is a medical doctor by profession.

You can contact Adeshola Ezeokoli, although she cannot respond personally to all correspondence, she would love to get your feedback.

Dr. Adeshola Ezeokoli
Kingsword Ministries International
3323 West Cermak Road
Chicago
Illinois 60623
USA

E-mail: **shola.ezeokoli@yahoo.com**

Website: **www.sholashade.wordpress.com**

Please include your testimony of help received from this book when you write. Your prayer requests are welcome.

You can order additional copies of this book @

www.amazon.com

www.GodKulturepublishing.com

or by mail through the postal address above.

OTHER BOOK BY THE AUTHOR

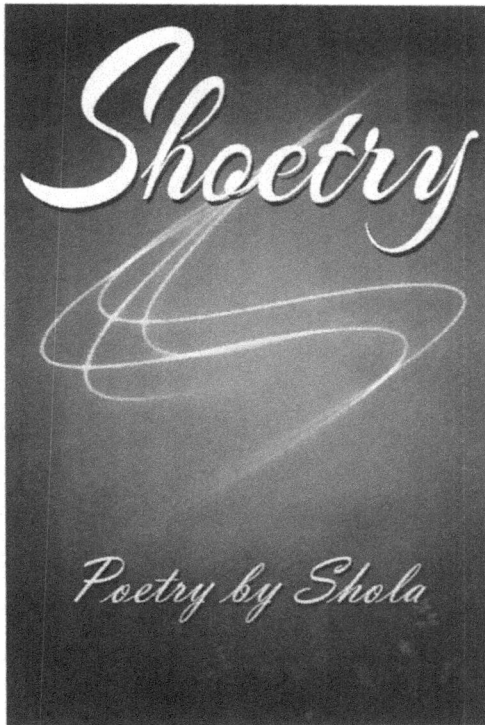

The point of this book is mainly to inspire people through the art form of poetry. It attempts to bring God-themes to life through free verse and rhymes. There are poems on the love of God, diligence, consistency, purpose, romantic love, fruit of the spirit, and many others.

It is an easy read, and I hope that as you read this book, the various topics represented will be brought home to your heart in a different way, and that you will enjoy them.

www.ingramcontent.com/pod-product-compliance
Lightning Source LLC
Chambersburg PA
CBHW060414050426
42449CB00009B/1967